INTEGRATED AND COMPREHENSIVE PROBLEMS IN TAXATION

By Anu Varadharajan

Tulane University

cognella
academic publishing

Bassim Hamadeh, CEO and Publisher
Michael Simpson, Vice President of Acquisitions
Jamie Giganti, Managing Editor
Miguel Macias Graphic Designer
Angela Kozlowski, Acquisitions Editor
Michelle Piehl Project Editor
Alexa Lucido, Licensing Coordinator

First published in the United States of America in 2015 by Cognella, Inc.

ISBN: 978-1-5165-5290-0

cognella academic publishing

www.cognella.com 800-200-3908

CONTENTS

CASEBOOK FOR PRINCIPLES OF TAXATION

This case book is a result of several years of teaching an introductory course in taxation to undergraduate accountancy students. Typically these students take only one tax class before graduating and heading on to careers in accounting. Therefore there is a lot of pressure on the students and faculty to ensure that students are up to speed in working with tax laws—especially in "real world" situations.

As a practitioner turned academic, I have always taught with a practical approach to tax. These cases came about because of frustrations in the classroom when students were unable to synthesize information in prior chapters as they progressed along in the course. Unfortunately, when they become tax practitioners, clients are going to give them information in phases, disorganized formats, and ask them for advice based on their whole tax posture. This feature is the biggest advantage of these tax cases.

These cases help develop the skills needed to determine the tax liability for individual taxpayers as well as the tax consequences of transactions involving property transactions.

HOW TO USE THIS BOOK

Instructors can use these cases to test student's understanding in applying concepts learned in one chapter while building on concepts learned on previous chapters.Weaknesses are highlighted when students attempt these cases—particularly understanding how various rules interact with each other to affect the tax liability of taxpayers.

A common weakness for students is with respect to property transactions. Depreciation and the Section 179 expenses tend to throw students for a loop. While students are able to determine cost recovery using MACRS tables, again, a weakness for understanding and demonstrating how the cost recovery rules work throughout the lifecycle of a long-term asset is a common frustration for students. The cases on property transactions address these issues.

STUDENTS

I encourage students to use these cases to really test their understanding of the concepts, figure out where they need additional practice and to demonstrate to themselves their complete understanding of the fundamental tax concepts for individual taxpayers.

CASE 1

Darren Jacobs

LEARNING OBJECTIVES

This case will help students evaluate their comprehension of the following concepts:

- Items included as taxable income
- Items excluded as taxable income
- Deductions for AGI
- Who can be claimed as dependent
- Filing status
- Calculating taxable income
- Calculating tax liability

Darren Jacobs, forty years old, is a music teacher at Champion High School. He also has a private studio where he teaches music to students in the community. Darren feels that his tax position is getting too complicated to handle himself, so he wants you to help him. The facts are listed below:

Salary	$60,000
Studio tuition	$12,000
Lottery winnings	$1,000
Interest income (First Midwest Bank)	$500
Income from Treasury bills	$800
Inheritance	$10,000
Gift made to his two nephews	$10,000
Qualified dividends	$2,400
Loss on sale of his personal car	($2,800)
Child support received from his ex-wife	$15,000
Capital loss carried forward from 2013	($9,500)

Darren also tells you about the people who depend on him:

- Jonathan, age fifteen, his son, who lives with him. Jonathan earns $1,000 from part-time jobs and is a full-time student at Champion High School.
- Jeremy, twenty-seven years old, his younger brother, is a graduate student at Eastern University. Jeremy earns $8,000 from summer internship and receives $12,000 in scholarship toward his tuition and books. Darren gives Jeremy $300 per month to help him with his expenses.
- Patty, Darren's mother, lives by herself, one hundred miles away. Darren, his two sisters, and their aunt support Patty equally. If he can, Darren would like to claim Patty as his dependent for 2014.
- Maxine, Darren's fiancée, moved in with him in November 2014. She is also a music teacher in the same school, and they plan to get married in January 2015.
- Darren's daughter, Dotty, is nineteen years old. She lives at home in the basement. She earned $4,500 in 2014 as a model. She plans to start cosmetology school in 2015 and is fully supported by Darren for all her needs.

ASSIGNMENT

For 2014, determine Darren's

a. Gross income
b. AGI
c. Dependents (provide clear explanations as to why each person qualifies or does not qualify as a dependent)
d. Filing status
e. Taxable income (assume that Darren chooses to take the standard deduction)
f. Tax liability

Bonus:

Calculate the standard deduction each dependent will claim on his or her tax return, if applicable.

CASE 2

Jack and Jill Taylor

LEARNING OBJECTIVES

This case will help students evaluate their comprehension of the following concepts discussed:

- Items included as taxable income
- Items excluded as taxable income
- Deductions for AGI
- Who can be claimed as a dependent
- Filing status
- Calculating taxable income
- Calculating tax liability—includes phase-out calculations for personal exemptions
- Determining average and marginal tax rates

Jack and Jill Taylor live on a hill in Texas. The Taylors work as engineers for Rainbow Construction Inc. For 2014, they expect to receive the following sources of income.

Salary	$303,200
Dividends	$50,000
Inheritance	$35,000

The Taylors expect the following payments in 2014:

Alimony paid by Jack to his ex-wife Julia	$18,000
Their itemized deductions are expected to be	$36,500

Additionally, the Taylors expect the following to happen in 2014:

- They will celebrate their twentieth wedding anniversary this year.
- Their twenty-one-year-old daughter, Julie, is in college, out of state. Julie will earn $3,500 as an intern over the summer, and Jack and Jill will pay another $5,500 for her expenses this year.
- Jill's fifty-year-old aunt also lives with them. Jill's aunt has no income and is fully supported by Jack and Jill.

ASSIGNMENT

For 2014, determine:

a. The Taylors' gross income
b. The Taylors' AGI
c. The Taylors' number of dependents
d. The number of personal exemptions the Taylors can claim
e. The Taylors' taxable income
f. The Taylors' tax liability
g. The marginal and average tax rates for the Taylors

CASE 3

Tim Green

LEARNING OBJECTIVES

This case will help students evaluate their comprehension of the following concepts:

- Tax treatment of annuity payments
- Determining income for an accrual basis taxpayer
- Treatment of damage payments
- Related party transactions
- Nondeductible items
- Treatment of vacation/rental property
- Calculating taxable income
- Calculating tax liability

Timmy Green is sixty-six years old. In preparing his 2014 tax return, he informs you of the following:

a. He bought an annuity for $150,000 when he turned sixty-five. The annuity pays $24,000 per year for the rest of his life. His life expectancy is eighty years.

b. Timmy owns a painting business and is an accrual basis taxpayer. The following are his receipts and payments for 2014:

2014 receipts	$170,000
Receipts related to 2013 projects	25,000
Wages	40,000
Supplies	15,000
Insurance payments due, not paid	3,000
Miscellaneous expenses	2,000
Income earned in 2014, not received	35,000

c. Jimmy (his son) gave him $10,000 as a birthday gift.

d. Timmy fell from a ladder while painting and was injured. He sued the ladder company for negligence and was awarded $50,000 in compensatory damages and $15,000 for lost wages.

e. Timmy sold his antique grandfather clock to his son Jimmy for $30,000. Timmy paid $38,000 for this clock.

f. Timmy paid $3,000 to the local government to lobby members of the city legislature.

g. In December 2013, Timmy bought a home in Steamboat Spring, Colorado. He paid $400,000 ($100,000 of his own money and $300,000 through a loan). He is not sure how to use this property in 2013. He knows that his expenses will be as follows:

Mortgage interest	$15,000
Property taxes	10,000
Utilities	2,400
Depreciation	4,300

Timmy has three options:

i. Use it for personal purposes the entire year
ii. Use it for personal purposes for sixty days and rent it for the remaining ten months, with rental income of $20,000
iii. Use it for personal purposes for twelve days and rent it out for the remaining days of the year, with rental income of $22,000

h. Timmy's best friend from high school, Will, lost everything in a tornado and moved in with Timmy on January 1, 2014. Will does not work and is fully supported by Timmy.

ASSIGNMENT

For 2014, determine Timmy's

a. Gross income
b. AGI
c. Dependents (provide clear explanations as to why each person qualifies or does not qualify as a dependent)
d. Filing status
e. Taxable income (assume that he chooses to take the standard deduction)
f. Tax liability

Bonus:

Determine the tax consequences to Timmy if he decides to use the house in Colorado under all three scenarios. Use the Bolton method and the IRS method for the mixed-use scenario.

CASE 4

Amber Graham

LEARNING OBJECTIVES

This case will help students evaluate their comprehension of the following concepts:

- Business expenses
- Investigating expenses
- Treatment of casualty loss of business and personal use property
- Deductions from AGI
- Filing status
- Calculate taxable income
- Calculate tax liability

Amber Graham is a self-employed interior decorator. She consults with you regarding her 2012 tax return and provides you with the following information.

1. On July 1, 2013, she was hired by Coral Industries to design their latest hotel. It is a twenty four month project that must be completed by June 30, 2015. Amber received $108,000 on July 1, 2013 as payment for the entire project.

2. She earned/incurred the following from her business for 2014:

Income:	$120,000
Expenses:	
License fee	$ 500
Trade publications	600
Supplies	30,000
Conventions	5,000
Secretary Salary	25,000
Postage	500
Legal/Attorney fees	8,000
Transportation	8,000 miles*
Speeding ticket	200
Parking fines	120

*Assume Amber uses the standard mileage rate to calculate expenses related to her car. She used her personal car for business trips also but carefully recorded the miles she travelled on each trip.

3. Amber sued an unhappy client for defamation and was awarded $80,000 in compensatory damages.

4. In 2014, Amber bought Divine Lighting, a local company that specializes in high-end lighting for homes and businesses. She spent $45,000 in investigating the business before buying it. She decided to expense the acquisition costs.

5. Amber's business was flooded during a heavy rainstorm. She sustained damages wherein her basis was $15,000 and insurance reimbursed her $10,000. Amber stored some personal property in her business that was also destroyed. Her basis in the property was $30,000, and the reduction in fair market value was $25,000. She was not reimbursed by insurance for her personal property.

6. Amber's twenty-year-old niece, Ruby, lives with her and is fully supported by Amber. Ruby is a full-time student at Parkland College.

ASSIGNMENT

For 2014, calculate Amber's

a. Income from her business
b. Gross Income
c. Deductions for AGI
d. Taxable Income
e. Tax liability

Bonus:

What is Amber received $250,000 as damages in 2014? How would your answer change then? What additional items do you need to consider in your calculations?

CASE 5

The Swoons

LEARNING OBJECTIVES

This case will help students evaluate their comprehension of the following concepts:

- Hobby activities
- Itemized deductions: medical expenses, mortgage expenses, charitable contributions, interest expenses, and miscellaneous expenses
- Deductions from AGI
- Filing status
- Calculating taxable income
- Calculating tax liability

Edward Swoon is employed by IBM. Bella Swoon, his wife, is a teacher. Their combined W-2 wages for 2014 are $260,000. IBM withheld $36,500 in federal income tax payments and $11,245 in state income tax payments. For 2014, the Swoons also had the following items:

- They contributed $8,200 to various charities. They had $5,000 of charitable contributions carried over from 2010.
- Bella incurred $200 in qualified educator expenses, which were not reimbursed.
- They paid $12,380 in real estate taxes on their home.
- They paid $17,500 as interest on the acquisition debt of their home.
- On February 1, 2014, they applied for a home equity loan of $125,000, when their equity was $135,000. For ease of calculation, assume that the interest is determined at 7% of the outstanding balance as of December 31, 2014, and payments are made only once per year—on December 31, 2014.
- The Swoons support both Bella's father (David Currant) and Edward's grandmother (Sylvia Swoon).
  - o David is seventy-five years old and is in reasonable health. Since David's wife passed away, Bella invited her father to move in with them, but he decided to move to an assisted living community so that he can be around other people his age. The Swoons pay $30,000 per year for David's stay at the home.
  - o Sylvia is ninety years old and in extremely poor health—she suffers from Alzheimer's and various ailments and needs constant care. Sylvia is also at an assisted living community, where nurses look after her around the clock. The Swoons would not be able to provide the care Sylvia needs and, therefore, pay $25,000 per year for her care and stay at the assisted living center.
- Edward has a passion for blacksmithing and makes beautiful knives and daggers. He sells them at the local arts festival and makes them to order for friends as gifts. He earns about $3,000 per year from selling knives and incurs $3,800 in expenses.
- The Swoons incurred $5,500 in various expenses (e.g., safety deposit box, accountant fees, subscriptions).
- The Swoons adopted a baby girl in March 2014. (Ignore all adoption-related expenses for now.)

ASSIGNMENT

For 2014, calculate/determine the Swoon's

a. Gross income
b. Deductions for AGI
c. Deductions from AGI
d. Filing status
e. Taxable income
f. Tax liability
g. Tax due/refund

Bonus:

What would your answer be if the Swoons earned $320,000 for 2014?

CASE 6

Tax Return Preparation

LEARNING OBJECTIVES

This case allows students to demonstrate their knowledge with respect to the following areas of individual tax return preparation. Based on students' performance on this case, tax faculty should be able to identify specific areas of weaknesses in comprehension of fundamental concepts as well as associated calculations.

a. Prepare Form 1040, including relevant schedules, for a taxpayer
b. Articulate the flow of information across several schedules
c. Determine sources of taxable, excluded income and deductions for AGI
d. Determine the impact of capital gains and losses
e. Demonstrate an understanding of various limitation rules related to AGI
f. Determine the appropriate use of itemized versus standard deduction
g. Determine whether a taxpayer has qualified dependents
h. Determine a taxpayer's filing status

BONUS OBJECTIVE

Provide basic tax planning ideas to a taxpayer depending on the facts provided in the tax return as well as the outcome of the tax return preparation

ASSIGNMENT

- Please use the information below to prepare a 2014 individual income tax return with any required attachments or schedules.
- All forms can be obtained from the IRS's website at www.irs.gov. You will need the following forms and schedules:

Form 1040	Schedule A	Schedule B
Schedule D	Form 8949	Publication 972
Form 1040 instructions		

- You may also use the software found in your textbook, but be careful when using any software, in that the output is actually what you want (remember: garbage in, garbage out).
- Turn in all relevant completed forms and schedules, and any calculations if they are not already apparent in the form. Please organize them in the following order:
  - o Form 1040
  - o Schedule A
  - o Schedule B
  - o Schedule D
  - o Form 8949
  - o Calculations for
    - ▪ Qualified dividends (from 1040 Instructions)
    - ▪ Child tax credit (from Publication 972)

Bonus:

After reviewing the Shakespeares' return, what tax planning strategies would you suggest?

FACTS

William (age forty-five) and Anne (age forty) Shakespeare are married and file a joint tax return. William is preparing the tax return. They reside at 10 Longfellow Place, Boston, Massachusetts 02114, phone number (617) 244-1000, with their two children and William's mother, Cordelia. Their social security numbers are as follows:

William	234-55-9988
Anne	901-22-6677
Romeo	112-34-0021
Juliet	030-73-8209
Cordelia	567-89-2413

1. William applies any overpayment of federal income tax to their 2015 estimated tax.

2. Employee compensation information:

William Shakespeare:

W2 wages	$220,000
Federal income tax withheld	$38,000
Social security tax withheld	$10,300
Medicare tax withheld	$3,340
State tax withheld	$15,300

Anne Shakespeare:

W2 wage	$120,400
Federal income tax withheld	$13,900
Social security tax withheld	$6,400
Medicare tax withheld	$2,400
State tax withheld	$9,800

3. Interest expense:
   The Shakespeares' acquisition debt on the house in Cambridge, Massachusetts, is $650,000. Their records show that they paid $50,000 in mortgage interest and $15,235 in property taxes.

4. Interest income reported on 1099-INT:
   a. Bank of America $1,300
   b. Interest income from tax-free Massachusetts municipal bonds $1,700

5. The Shakespeares also received qualified dividends, as follows:
   a. Lear Corp. $3,500
   b. Othlo Inc. $2,000

6. On April 1, 2014, the Shakespeares bought a vacation condo in Boca Raton, Florida, for $400,000. They stayed in the condo from June 1 through July 30, 2014, and rented it out from May 1 through 25 and September 1 through December 31, 2014. Their income and expenses associated with this condo are as follows:

Income	$8,000
Property taxes	$4,325
Mortgage interest	$12,380
Utilities	$2,325
Repairs/maintenance	$425
Depreciation	$5,152

   William uses the Bolton method to determine the net income from such property.

7. Anne is an amateur photographer. She sells two or three of her photographs at the local art market once per quarter. Occasionally, her friends pay her to take photographs of their families. In 2014, she earned $3,000 from her photography. She spent $1,000 in supplies, and $2,500 in printing, framing, and so forth.

8. William Shakespeare pays alimony and child support to his first wife and his daughter, Desdemona, in the sum of $30,000 and $18,000 respectively. The daughter does not live with the Shakespeares, and this is the last year in which William will have to pay child support, as his daughter will turn twenty-one in 2015.

9. The Shakespeares report the following capital transactions for 2014:

# of shares	Company	Acquired	Sold/ worthless	Sales price	Basis
200	PPR	4/1/2012	8/1/2014		2,000
2,500					
1000	DRMA	2/2/2009	12/3/2014		9,000
8,000					
1000	HVI	1/31/2008	12/31/2014	0	7,000

10. Being of a generous nature, the Shakespeares contribute to several qualified charities as follows:

Misc. cash contributions	$400
St. Paul Church	$1,300
Charles River Fire Dept.	$2,600

The Shakespeares also traveled to New York City to volunteer their time for Habitat for Humanity. They spent $3,000 for lodging for one month, $2,100 for meals, and $1,100 in transportation to New York. Their lost income from this month of charitable work is estimated to be $9,500.

(Note: The Shakespeares need not fill out Form 8283 along with Schedule A.)

11. Medical expenses:
Cordelia Shakespeare, William's mother, has a very bad heart that requires constant care. The Shakespeares spent $27,300 on her care in 2014 and are debating whether they should put her in a nursing home that costs $40,000 per year. The home will provide Cordelia with all the medical care that she needs, which the Shakespeares cannot provide for her at this time.

12. Misc. deductions subject to the 2% floor:
   a. Estate planning attorney's fees $1,800
   b. Publications $200
   c. Safe deposit box rentals $100

Other Notes

Ignore the alternative minimum tax.
Ignore any tax credits other than the (regular) child tax credit.
You do not need to prepare the Illinois tax return.
Remember that the return has to be signed and dated!

Round any numbers to whole dollars (including depreciation, self-employment tax, the total tax, etc.).

CASE 7

Dew Organics

LEARNING OBJECTIVES

Do students understand the concept of § 179—specifically,

a. How to apply the asset limitation?
b. How to apply the taxable income limitation?
c. How to apply the annual dollar limitation to all the assets bought in the year?

Dew Organics, a calendar-year company, started doing business in January 2014. It made the following acquisitions:

Asset	Date placed in service	Cost
Furniture	2/14/2014	$30,000 (Note: $10,000 was secondhand furniture)
Equipment	4/15/2014	$80,000
Computer	5/10/2014	$50,000

Dew calculates its start-up costs to be $40,000. It also acquired customer lists for $84,000 in January 2014.

a. Assume that Dew Organics wants to maximize all property-related deduction.
b. The CFO, Mia Kerr, is not sure whether taxable income will be $20,000 or $80,000.

Based on the above information, determine the total cost recovery that Dew Organics can claim for 2014.

CASE 8

C-U Multipurpose

LEARNING OBJECTIVES

What does this case achieve?

1. Do students understand the concept of § 179—specifically,
   a. How to apply the asset limitation?
   b. How to apply the taxable income limitation?
   c. How to apply the annual dollar limitation to all the assets bought in the year?.

2. How to prepare Form 4562 accurately:
   a. Reflect the § 179 limitations in Form 4562
   b. Show the interaction for depreciation calculations for assets acquired in previous years and the current year
   c. Demonstrate an understanding of all aspects of cost recovery

C-U Multipurpose Inc. (federal ID: 7393124409) is a company that has been operating since June 1, 2010. Given below are details of assets that have been placed into service by C-U Multipurpose since it began operations.

ASSET	DATE PLACED	BASIS/COST
Asset A (office furniture)	3/12/2012	$12,500
Asset B (agricultural machine)	8/15/2012	$120,000
Asset C (computers and peripherals)	10/10/2014 (acquired 10/1/2014)	$350,000
Asset D (tractor unit for the road)	11/30/2014 (acquired 10/31/2014)	$180,000
Asset E (patent acquired)	10/1/2010	$78,000
Start-up costs	6/1/2010 (date business started)	$69,800
Goodwill (self-created)	6/1/2010 (date business started)	$200,000

C-U Multipurpose does not believe that 2014 will be a very profitable year and expects its taxable income before §179 expenses to be $100,000. Assume that any elected §179 or bonus depreciation expense amounts are claimed on assets related to tax year 2012.

INSTRUCTIONS AND DELIVERABLES

This is an *individual* assignment. Please do not discuss this assignment with anyone else (either within the class or outside the class).

ASSIGNMENT

1. A brief explanation of
   a. The conventions used
   b. Cost recovery not taken for any asset
   c. The amount and treatment of any unused §. 179 expense (if any)

2. Calculate the 2014 cost recovery deduction for C-U Multipurpose Inc. Ensure that your calculation has the following:
   a. §tion 179 expense
   b. Bonus depreciation
   c. MACRS amounts for all applicable assets
   d. Amortization of all applicable assets

3. Complete Form 4562 for this taxpayer for the year ended December 31, 2012. Ignore Part V of this form.

CASE 9

Rex Winston

LEARNING OBJECTIVES

This case will help students evaluate their comprehension of the following concepts:

- Treatment of property received as inheritance
- Converting property from personal use to business use
- Depreciating business use real property
- Determining gain and loss on disposal of personal and business property
- Treatment of gain on disposal of § 121 property
- Netting of gains and losses
- Calculating taxable income
- Calculating tax liability

On January 15, 2010, Rex Winston's grandmother died, and as her sole heir, Rex inherited the following:

a. A house valued at $500,000, which his grandmother bought for $100,000. The house is located in Gary, Indiana.
b. An apartment in Chicago worth $300,000, which his grandmother bought for $200,000.
c. An Ansel Adams photograph worth $300,000, bought for $5,000 in 1940.
d. An antique pistol that was used in the Revolutionary War. No one knows how Rex's grandmother received it, but it is estimated to be worth $750,000.
e. Ten thousand shares in Microsoft, worth $30 each on January 15, 2010.

Rex decided to move into the Chicago condo on March 1, 2010, and uses it as his principal residence. He rented the house on March 1, 2010, which is when he received the house. He earns $2,000 as rental income per month from this house.

On March 1, 2014, Rex decides to sell all of the items received in his inheritance. He received $400,000 for the house in Indiana, $600,000 for the apartment in Chicago, and $350,000 for the Ansel Adams photograph and $850,000 for the antique pistol (both are collector's items), and he sold the Microsoft shares for $27 per share.

He also works as an engineer, earning $120,000. He has no other sources of income. He is single and has no dependents. In 2014, he paid $800 in real estate taxes on his Chicago condo. He expects to pay $3,400 in Illinois state taxes for 2014.

He also has $55,000 of capital losses carried forward from prior years.

ASSIGNMENT

a. Determine Rex's basis in each property received in 2010.
b. Determine Rex's basis in each property when it was sold in 2014.
c. Determine the gain or loss and the character when the property was sold in 2014.
d. For 2014, calculate Rex's taxable income and tax liability.

CASE 10

Burgundy

LEARNING OBJECTIVES

What does this case achieve?

1. Do students understand the concept of § 1245 property in terms of the following:
   a. How the depreciation recapture rules work?
   b. How to apply the recapture amounts?
   c. How to re-characterize the income and losses?

2. How rules work for the capital loss carried forward.

The chart below describes the assets used by the Burgundy Company (a sole proprietorship), which were sold on December 31, 2014.

a. Compute the gain or loss from each asset disposition and determine the character of the gain or loss. Use the table below to show your calculations.

ASSET	ACQUIRED	SOLD	COST	DEPRECIATION	SALE PRICE
Stamping machine	3/10/2010	8/10/2014	$40,000	$29,736	$32,000
Printing press	2/12/2011	7/23/2014	$80,000	$18,838	$90,000
Tractor	5/16/2012	11/12/2014	$52,000	$52,000	$30,000
Overhead crane	01/02/2014	12/10/2014	$74,000	$10,000	$80,000

b. Burgundy's capital loss carry-forward schedule is given below. It did not have any un-recaptured Sec. 1231 losses from prior years.
December 31, 2013: $5,000
December 31, 2011: $0
December 31, 2010: $15,000

i. Compute the net capital loss carried forward as to 2015.
ii. What planning strategy would you recommend to Burgundy to enable it to use its net capital loss carry-forwards?

CASE 11

Swanky

LEARNING OBJECTIVES

This case will help students evaluate their comprehension of the following concepts:

- Treatment of like-kind exchanges
- Determining gain or loss on the disposal of business property
- §1231 un-recaptured losses
- Netting of gains and losses

SWANKY INC. PROPERTY TRANSACTIONS

Depreciation, Sale/Exchange, §1231, §1245, Netting, LTCG

Swanky Inc. is a helmet manufacturer, in business since 1998. It makes all types of helmets—for adults, kids, bicycles, motorcycles, skating, and so on. For the year 2014, Swanky Inc. entered into the following transactions:

a. It sold machinery that was fully depreciated for $250,000. The machine ("Machine S1") was bought on July 1, 1998, for $200,000.

b. Swanky exchanged a welding machine ("Machine S2"; basis of $110,000, bought for $250,000, FMV $125,000) with Lanky Inc. Lanky's machine has a fair market value of $100,000. Therefore, Lanky gave the remainder as cash to Swanky.

c. In January 2014, Swanky's purchasing manager, Todd Lofty, bought a stamping machine ("Machine S3") for applying the Swanky logo to helmets, for $45,000. In July, an internal investigation revealed that Todd was taking cutbacks from suppliers and that the stamping machine was of a very poor quality. Swanky fired Lofty and sold the stamping machine for $35,000.

d. On its 2010, 2011, and 2012 tax returns, Swanky deducted $5,000, $17,000, and $13,000 as §1231 losses.

e. Between 2006 and 2008, Swanky's market-savvy CFO, Rob Liddy, invested in several blue-chip stocks, investment-grade land, and so on. In 2014, Rob sold all these investments, yielding the following gains and losses:
    Gain on sale of stock: $24, 000
    Loss on sale of stock: $13,000
    Gain on sale of land (A): $120,000
    Loss on sale of land (B): $36,000

f. In 2014, Rob also made the following transactions for Swanky:
    IBM stock: bought on 1/14/2014 and sold on 5/25/2014. Net gain: $14,500.
    GE stock: bought on 2/11/2014 and sold on 8/15/2014. Net loss: $8,300.

g. Swanky also has the following net capital loss carry-forwards from prior tax years:
    2008 ($15,000)
    2009 ($8,000)
    2010 ($27,000)
    2011 ($11,000)
    2012 ($13,000)
    2013 ($35,000)

Using a flowchart, show the impact of these transactions and the net capital gain or loss for 2014, as well as the amounts carried forward to 2015, if any.

www.ingramcontent.com/pod-product-compliance
Lightning Source LLC
LaVergne TN
LVHW060250011026
849161LV00011B/2685